MOTHER TERESA OF CALCUTTA

CTS Children's Books

Contents

The Light of God in the darkness of the world 3

Little Agnes Gonxha 4

I want to be a missionary 6

Sister Teresa... Mother Teresa 8

A special calling 10

Missionary of charity 12

With Jesus among the poor 14

The face of the suffering Jesus 16

Like a tiny seed 18

Blessed Teresa of Calcutta 20

Some thoughts of Mother Teresa 21

An image of Mother Teresa 23

A prayer 24

Text by Elena Pascoletti
Illustrations by Giusi Capizzi
Translated by Pierpaolo Finaldi

Mother Teresa of Calcutta: Published 2013 by The Incorporated Catholic Truth Society, 40-46 Harleyford Road, London SE11 5AY. Tel: 020 7640 0042; Fax: 020 7640 0046; www.cts-online.org.uk. Copyright © 2013 The Incorporated Catholic Truth Society in this English-language edition.

ISBN: 978 1 86082 847 8 CTS Code CH 45

Translated from the original Italian Edition **Madre Teresa di Calcutta** - ISBN 978-88-6124-164-0, published by Il Pozzo di Giacobbe, Gruppo Editoriale S.R.L., Cortile San Teodoro, 3, 91100 Trapani (TP), Italy © 2012 Il Pozzo di Giacobbe.

THE LIGHT OF GOD IN THE DARKNESS OF THE WORLD

Calcutta (or Kolkata) is a big and crowded city in the Bengal region of Eastern India. In the twentieth century the city went through difficult and violent times. As a British colony, Calcutta was involved in the Second World War and there was a great conflict between the city's Muslim and Hindu inhabitants. It also suffered a great famine. The city was crowded with desperately poor workers who flocked there, hoping to make a living. In the streets of this city worked a tiny woman who was humble and full of energy. She carried a rosary and was always smiling… Her name was Mother Teresa and she was a missionary who worked to show God's love for everyone, especially for the poorest of the poor. But her amazing story began very far away…

LITTLE AGNES GONXHA

Skopje is an ancient and important city in Serbia, in a very mountainous area of Europe called the Balkans. There, a couple called Nikola and Drana Bojaxhiu lived together with their children. They were a well-off Catholic family who came from Albania. Nikola, the father, was a well-known and successful merchant. He spoke many languages and often had to travel for business. Drana looked after the children and the house which was always full of other people too. She was very generous and made sure that the poor and lonely were always welcome in their house.

On 26th August 1910 a little girl was born to the Bojaxhiu family. The very next day she was baptised and named Agnes Gonxha.

Agnes Gonxha was only eight when her father returned from a long journey. He fell sick and died in the hospital. Suddenly the family was left without a father and without much money but they remained peaceful and generous. Gonxha's mother was a woman of great faith and determination. She earned money for the family by sewing and embroidering dresses so that her children never went hungry.

Despite their poverty they made sure there was always enough food to give to those who were in greater need and they often looked after an old and sick lady who had been abandoned by her family. For little Gonxha, her family home was like a school where she learned to have a deep and caring love towards the poor.

I WANT TO BE A MISSIONARY

From the moment of her First Holy Communion, Agnes Gonxha felt a great love for Jesus in her heart. She wanted everyone in the world to know about him and to love him. Her family prayed together every day and went to church in the Parish of the Sacred Heart in Skopje where all the Albanian Catholics gathered. Agnes Gonxha loved music and sang in the church choir together with her sister Aga. When she was 12 she began to feel called by God to the religious life.

In her heart she asked, "Jesus, is this what you want from me?"

She spoke with the priest who led the community in Skopje and he gave her a clear and simple answer: "The right path is where you will find joy!"

Agnes Gonxha was fascinated by the letters that arrived in the parish, which were written by Jesuit missionaries working in Calcutta. She felt more and more strongly that this was the life to which God was calling her. Yes, she wanted to be a missionary! As soon as she was eighteen years old she told her mother that she wanted to join the Sisters of Loreto who had a mission in India.

At the beginning Drana was not very enthusiastic about the idea: she knew that Gonxha would need to be very brave. In the end she gave her blessing and gave Gonxha some words of wisdom that remained always in her heart: "Put your hand in the hand of Jesus and walk with him alone. Go forward always, because if you look back you will return."

SISTER TERESA... MOTHER TERESA

On the 26th September 1928, Agnes Gonxha left her house and began a long journey across Europe to the Sisters of Loreto in Ireland. She was given the new name of Mary Teresa in honour of Therese of Lisieux, one of her favourite saints. After a few weeks she left on a ship to India, to the mission she had always wanted. She arrived in Calcutta on the 6th January 1929 and was sent to a convent in Darjeeling in the foothills of the Himalayas for two years to be prepared for the religious life.

After her first vows (especially solemn promises) Teresa was sent back to Calcutta where the Sisters of Loreto had opened a school. All girls, whether they were English, Indian, poor or orphans could study there. Teresa was their new history and geography teacher.

In May 1937 Sister Teresa made her perpetual vows and became Mother Teresa, Bride of Jesus, consecrated to him forever. She promised to do whatever Jesus asked of her and she offered every sacrifice to Jesus with love. She was a diligent nun and teacher and was a great example of humility and prayer. She made sure that even the smallest things were done to the best of her ability.

A SPECIAL CALLING

Every Sunday when she was not teaching, Mother Teresa would spend her time visiting the poor who lived near the convent. She had nothing to give them but only a radiant smile and the simple joy of bringing the love of Jesus to those who needed it most. On the 10th September 1946 Mother Teresa was travelling on a train from Calcutta to Darjeeling for a short time of rest and spiritual exercises. Something unexpected happened on the train that would change her life forever...

She felt a 'calling within her calling'.

Jesus was asking her for another act of love. He wanted her to leave the sisters of Loreto to work in the streets serving the poorest of the poor. She could hear within her the cry of Jesus on the cross when he said: "I thirst". Jesus helped her to understand that his thirst was for every person to experience his love and to love him in return.

Mother Teresa's mission among the poor was her answer to Jesus' cry. She would quench the infinite thirst of Jesus and bring the light of God to the smallest and the most miserable in Calcutta, to help them feel how much God loves them. She would have left immediately for her new work, but her superiors in the order and the Archbishop of Calcutta asked her to wait and pray to better understand God's will for her.

Mother Teresa was impatient to get started but waited in trust and obedience.

MISSIONARY OF CHARITY

Two years after her inspiration on the train Mother Teresa received permission from Rome to leave the Sisters of Loreto and work with the poor. On the 17th August 1948 with only 5 rupees in her hand, and dressed in a simple white Indian sari with blue borders, she walked through the gate of her beloved convent.

Even though she had wanted this more than anything else, Mother Teresa felt that it was a bigger sacrifice to leave the convent than it had been to leave her family all those years ago.

She felt small and daunted by such a huge task. But she heard Jesus' voice echoing in her ears and in her heart, saying: "Do not be afraid. I will be with you always. Trust in me with love, trust me completely!" The first thing she did was go to the hospital run by another order of nuns, in a place called Patna. There she learnt everything she would need to know to look after the sick and dying in Calcutta.

On the 21st December for the first time she headed to the slum areas of the city to the shacks and hovels where the poorest people lived. She tended people's wounds and washed the little children. In a small open space in the middle of the huts she began to teach people the Bengali alphabet by writing in the sand with a small stick.

WITH JESUS AMONG THE POOR

After a few months she was joined by another girl, and then another three. Some had been her pupils at the convent school and wanted to follow her example. In a short time the first little community of the Missionaries of Charity was born. The sisters took the three solemn promises called vows, which every religious takes: "of absolute poverty, angelic chastity and joyful obedience". To these three they added a fourth: "to serve the poorest of the poor".

Mother Teresa told her sisters, "To serve the poor, we must understand them. And to understand their poverty there is no other way than to experience it."

For this reason the Missionaries of Charity learnt the local language very well and shared their food and clothes with poor people who lived around them.

Early in the morning they would walk and pray in the streets of Calcutta, bringing Jesus' love to those who needed it most. They would find food and clothing for them, teach their children to read and write, and clean the dirtiest houses… all with a smile.

They had very little money to do all this work, but they saw day by day how God provided everything they needed, even the smallest things.

THE FACE OF THE SUFFERING JESUS

The city authorities could see how much poverty there was in Calcutta, so they helped the Missionaries to find a suitable place where they could welcome all the people they met in the streets. The sick and dying, lepers and abandoned children, people with no hope… In each person, Mother Teresa could see the face of the suffering Jesus. She loved Jesus and wanted to give him back his trust, his dignity and to see him smile again.

Many people were brought to the "Home for the Dying". They were picked up from the streets in a terrible condition and looked after by Mother Teresa's missionaries. Some were cured but most were simply looked after with love, washed, tended, and prayed with, each according to his own religion. Other houses were opened to look after the great number of handicapped or orphaned and abandoned children. Many were starving or simply not wanted by their families. Mother Teresa often said: "If you hear that a woman does not want to keep her child, persuade her to bring the child to me and I will love him, because he is a sign of the love of God."

LIKE A TINY SEED

Year after year, the work that God had entrusted to Mother Teresa grew and bore fruit, like a big tree that grows from a tiny seed.

Her order grew and was soon joined by an order for men, the Missionaries of Charity Brothers, and then came an order of contemplative Sisters and Brothers who spent all their time in prayer. Next came the Missionaries of Charity Fathers, which was founded for priests, while ordinary people who wanted to help in the Mission could join the Lay Missionaries of Charity.

They worked in every continent and in every country where the poor lived side by side with the rich, in big cities full of wealth.

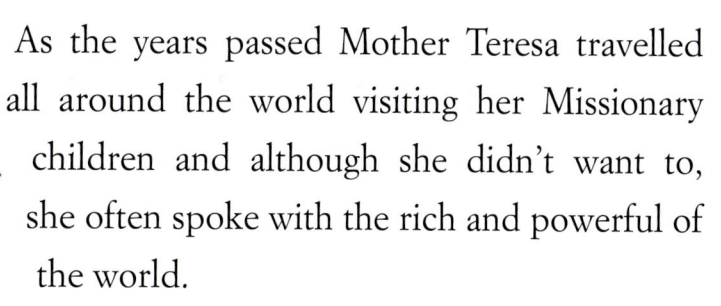

As the years passed Mother Teresa travelled all around the world visiting her Missionary children and although she didn't want to, she often spoke with the rich and powerful of the world.

She was respected and admired for her work and in 1979 was given the Nobel Peace Prize! Mother Teresa accepted it with great humility - not for herself, but for the Glory of God, and on behalf of the poor.

Soon afterwards a poor man came knocking on her door. He had heard about the Nobel Prize and decided to give the little money he had earned that day to help her work. Mother Teresa said that this was more important to her than the prize itself.

Mother Teresa died in Calcutta on the evening of the 5th September 1997. She was a true witness to the love of God for every creature and especially for the smallest and the weakest. Her message was simple, clear and courageous. It could be summed up in the last words of a poem she wrote... "Life is life: defend it!"

BLESSED TERESA OF CALCUTTA

Mother Teresa was beatified very quickly by Pope John Paul II. He knew her well and had always encouraged her in her work. The ceremony took place on the 9th October 2003 on World Mission Sunday, in front of a huge crowd of people.

The words from the Gospel that day echoed in everybody's heart, because Mother Teresa had lived those words completely: "I was hungry and you gave me to eat, I was thirsty and you gave me to drink… Whatever you did for the least of these little brothers of mine, you did it for me." (Mt 25:35,40)

The Church celebrates the feast of Blessed Teresa of Calcutta on the 5th September.

SOME THOUGHTS OF MOTHER TERESA

Peace begins with a smile.

I am a little pencil in the hand of a writing God who is sending a love letter to the world.

Love begins at home, and it is not how much we do that matters... but how much love we put into the things we do.

*Spread love everywhere you go.
Let no one ever come to you
without leaving happier.*

*We cannot do great things on this Earth,
only small things with great love.*

*Be the living expression of God's kindness:
kindness in your face, kindness in your eyes,
kindness in your smile.*

AN IMAGE OF MOTHER TERESA

A PRAYER

Dear Lord

Do you want my hands today

to help the poor and the sick and needy?

Lord I give you my hands.

Lord do you want my feet today

to visit those who have need of a friend?

Lord I give you my feet.

Lord do you want my voice today

to speak to those who need to hear a word of love?

Lord, take my voice.

Lord do you want my heart today

to love every human being

because they are a human being?

Lord today I give you my heart.

Amen.